HONORARY DOCTORATE
PROF. DR. RICHARD SPARKS

EREDOCTORAAT
PROF. DR. RICHARD SPARKS

ACTA FALCONIS
XXVI

HONORARY DOCTORATE
PROF. DR. RICHARD SPARKS

in honour of the 90th anniversary
of criminology (1929-2019) in Leuven

EREDOCTORAAT
PROF. DR. RICHARD SPARKS

ter ere van de 90ste verjaardag van
criminologische wetenschappen (1929-2019)
in Leuven

intersentia
Cambridge – Antwerp – Chicago

Intersentia Ltd
Sheraton House | Castle Park
Cambridge | CB3 0AX | United Kingdom
Tel.: +44 1223 370 170 | Fax: +44 1223 370 169
Email: mail@intersentia.co.uk
www.intersentia.com | www.intersentia.co.uk

Honorary Doctorate Prof. dr. Richard Sparks in honour of the 90th anniversary of criminology (1929-2019) in Leuven
Eredoctoraat Prof. Dr. Richard Sparks ter ere van de 90ste verjaardag van criminologische wetenschappen (1929-2019) in Leuven

ISBN 978-1-78068-867-1
D/2019/7849/73
NUR 820

British Library Cataloguing in Publication Data. A catalogue record for this book is available from the British Library.

Contents

Introduction on the Occasion of the Honorary Doctorate of Professor Richard Sparks

Bernard TILLEMAN
Dean of the Law Faculty, KU Leuven

Dear Rector,
Dear Honorary Doctors of the past and the future,
Dear Professors John Braithwaite and Richard Sparks,
Dear Honorary Rector,
Dear Fellow Deans,
Dear Ladies and Gentlemen,
Dear Colleagues,
Dear Students,
Dear Friends,

It is my privilege to welcome you, in the name of the Faculty, to this celebration on the occasion of the ninetieth anniversary of the Leuven Institute of Criminology. I would like to address a special welcome to our foreign guests as we are a very international company today. I'm particularly glad to welcome our honorary doctor John Braithwaite who specially flew over from Australia and our future honorary doctor, pro-dean Richard Sparks of Edinburgh Law School together with Marion, Tom, Rosie and Philip and other criminology colleagues from Argentina and the UK, a part of Europe with which both the University, the Faculty and our Institute of Criminology want to strengthen the ties, whatever the outcome may be of the ongoing political process that at least invites us to reflect critically about democratic politics, as we did in the conference preceding this academic ceremony.

We are all modern people. We know that all moments have the same fundamental characteristics. They are but points in a coordinated system. Modern science with its techniques and clocks can determine every moment precisely, always in the same, exact manner. And yet according to Herman De Dijn's latest book *Rituelen* we're not just modern people. We can't live in a neutral world, the world of science. In our social world not all places and moments are the same or equal. Your husband's, wife's or friend's birthday is only a number, and an arbitrary one at that, as it depends on the kind of calendar used. But don't you dare forget it and act as if it were a normal day like any other. The Faculty Board did not want to let the opportunity slip by to celebrate the ninetieth anniversary of its largest research unit. Within every community there are periodical interruptions of daily routine. There is normal time and time for celebration. Celebrations are collective events that confirm and draw attention to life and its most important events and transitions. For this purpose usual labour activities are interrupted for leisure time, as it is only during free time that such attention becomes possible. Time is stopped in order to draw attention to the essence of things, including time itself, namely the fact that we do not have full control. A celebration is an occasion to welcome new members, to commemorate important people or events so that they will help us and inspire us to live in the right way. With the presentation of an honorary doctorate the university confirms anew the importance of criminology for the future and expresses its appreciation for what the group of Leuven criminologists is doing today and has done in the past.

Ninety-one years ago Louis Braffort, renowned criminal lawyer, professor of criminal law and later also a principled president of the Bar Council, had a dream which he recorded in *une mémoire pour la fondation d'une école de sciences criminelles à l'université de Louvain*, which accords perfectly with the university's current mission statement: knowledge development at the service of humanity and society, with special attention for its most vulnerable members. Braffort was imbued with the doctrine of *défense sociale* which qualified crime as a social illness:

> *'C'est dans l'âme du criminel qui me livrait son secret comme à son confesseur ou dont je m'efforçais, malgré lui, de percer le mystère dans le tête à tête de mon cabinet d'avocat ou d'un parloir de prison, c'est en l'observant aux prises avec la justice aux cours des audiences répressives, c'est en interrogeant magistrats, avocats, experts en médecine mentale aumôniers et fonctionnaires des prisons que je me suis essayé à déchiffrer l'énigme de la criminalité'.*

Society must defend itself against this social illness but at the same time also employ all scientific means for the moral improvement and rehabilitation of the delinquent. The problem of criminality can't be approached exclusively from a legal perspective, but must be treated as a multidisciplinary phenomenon with psychiatric, psychological, moral and philosophical components. At the start, criminology was a science auxiliary to criminal law, an additional study for future criminal lawyers, doctors and senior officials of the judiciary who had to be educated so they could realise the ideals of *défense social* and arrive at an efficient and humane administration of criminal law. During its first forty years the staff of the Leuven School of Criminology consisted of leading criminal lawyers and forensic psychiatrists who had close ties with the prison sector. The modern Leuven Institute of Criminology has forgotten neither its historical roots nor its pioneers Braffort, De Greeff, Bondue and Dellaert: there is a structural connection with research in criminal law because the school is part of a joint research unit Criminal Law and Criminology and a lasting prominent presence of renowned psychiatrists – and at one time even anti-psychiatrists and (forensic) psychologists – in a multidisciplinary setting: lawyers, psychologists, sociologists and political scientists, specialists in public administration and criminologists.

From the sixties onwards, criminology, influenced by among others Lode Van Outrive, gradually became an autonomous critical social science based on empirical research. Its outlook was broadened from a focus on crime and criminals to research into the administration of criminal law: instead of clinically treating individuals, criminology began to critically question society itself. This led to the understanding that criminal law and the administration of criminal justice use a selective approach. Criminology is critical of power in its analysis of both the punitive reaction to criminal behaviour as well as the functioning of the institutions which give concrete shape to this reaction – the police, the judiciary and the prisons. What is special about the DNA of the Leuven School of Criminology is its attention to support for victims – victims of crimes, of traffic, of abuse within the church. Victimology was introduced as a research and educational domain by the late lamented Tony Peters. This brings us to restorative justice: a restorative approach within the administration of criminal justice that makes use of mediation between victims and perpetrators.

In 1968, under the influence of Dellaert and De Batselier, the Leuven School of Criminology was the first to launch a fully-fledged programme in criminology. 30 students enrolled for the first year; by now student numbers have risen to 1,164. These rising student numbers have also created room for more full-time professional researchers. Today, with 50 full-time equivalent, the research unit Criminal law and Criminology is the largest research unit in terms of direct government funding, and it also has a sizeable number of researchers with external funding.

The Leuven Institute of Criminology strives to play an active and critical part in the criminological field and in broader public debates related to its domains of expertise and wants to take up 'a visible, active and critical role in international and national criminologically relevant networks and organisations, in both academia and the world of policy'. An anniversary like today allows us to emphasise the societal impact of the criminological research conducted in Leuven. Through their research and participation in steering committees, committees for the preparation of policy, parliamentary investigation committees, policy bodies like the High Council for Justice, the criminologists of the university have an influence on Flemish and Belgian policy concerning safety, police, prisons, drugs, youth protection and special youth welfare, and counter-terrorism. The academic context offers possibilities to transcend the immediate policy context so as to develop a theoretical and critical criminology and conduct action research into novel experiments concerning the care for former detainees, prevention and restorative justice. Criminologists and their work indisputably contribute to the establishment of larger policy options such as the very progressive Basic Law for the Prison System and the Legal Position of Detainees. In the current climate, with its sometimes populist opinions of criminal law, their contribution is more than necessary. *Strafrecht ohne Kriminologie ist blind, Kriminologie ohne Strafrecht ist uferlos.*

A final development in criminology is the increasing internationalisation. There is a far-reaching internationalisation of traditional and new forms of crimes. Criminology is becoming more than a purely Western science, as it is also given a new interpretation on other continents. It is important that our students can follow this evolution. It is therefore to be applauded that the staff of the Leuven Institute of Criminology has become more international. Besides the Global Criminology professors, 25% of the current professors are not Belgian, with a serious Italian brain drain and also an Asian connection, through the half-Indonesian roots of our most recently appointed member of senior academic staff. In addition, we must encourage our students even more to participate in the Erasmus programme, and the latest developments in this respect are favourable. We are also hoping to embark on an international cooperation in the context of our Master in Criminology. It is good that on the occasion of the ninetieth anniversary we have reflected on internationalisation not only with all of the Belgian institutes for criminology in Flanders and Wallonia, but also with an international company of institutions invited by the two promotors of our honorary doctor.

Today we do not only celebrate the ninetieth anniversary of the Leuven School of Criminology. We also celebrate our ambition, our common goal to strive for excellent education and research. Education and research which are adapted to the needs of the 21st century, without neglecting, however, the continuous reflection upon our rich history that was the subject of the very challenging conference that preceded. Education and research which do not only serve our local society, but also embrace the international community. In short, a Faculty that is open to the world. I am very honoured to welcome Richard Sparks – an outstanding scholar who embodies the philosophy of the Leuven Institute of Criminology.

Laudatio for Professor Richard Sparks

Tom Daems and Stefaan Pleysier
Promotores doctor honoris causa

Leuven, 25 April 2019

Honourable Rector,
Your Excellencies,
Dear Colleagues,
Ladies and Gentlemen,
Dear Students,

In April 1901 Enrico Ferri, one of the key figures of the Italian School, gave a series of three lectures in Naples, on the positive school. Ferri was far from modest about the ambitions and future achievements of criminology: '… we believe that the study of the criminal, and the logical consequences therefrom, will bring about the complete transformation of human justice, not only as a theory laid down in scientific books, but also as a practical function applied every day to that living and suffering portion of humanity which has fallen into crime'. Enrico Ferri's firm belief in the transformative potential of the new 'science of the criminal' was shared by many and informed a wide-ranging international reform movement aimed at rethinking criminal law – *la défense sociale*. And, indeed, these developments would be pivotal in founding the first School of Criminology in Leuven in

1929. For Louis Braffort the School's principal goal was to teach and train professionals in such a way that they would understand the problem of crime 'beyond criminal law', in all its different dimensions.

Anno 2019 criminology – in Italy, Leuven or elsewhere – is very different from the time of Ferri or Braffort: contemporary criminology is probably less ambitious and perhaps it has lowered its expectations, but it is also different in terms of the research questions being addressed, the methodologies being applied, and the many ways in which it relates to criminal law, policy making and public debate. Criminology now moves from crime science to critical or cultural criminology, from feminist criminology to restorative or transitional justice, it covers sub-disciplines and areas as diverse as penology, policing studies, youth justice, victimology, situational crime prevention and forensic criminology. In 1950 the American-Swedish criminologist Thorsten Sellin could still argue that criminologists are 'kings without a country' but this has changed significantly: the number of students, degree programmes, research projects, academic journals, professional associations and conferences is impressive – the institutionalisation of criminology seems to be an accomplished fact.

Over the past three decades Professor Richard Sparks has played a key role in reinventing criminology and making it into an independent and thriving academic discipline within a European research context – and beyond. Professor Sparks not only contributed to this collective endeavour by his own empirical and theoretical work but also by reflecting upon the field of criminology as a whole – a challenging task which has become increasingly important in our current times. Indeed, the growth of criminology across the globe goes hand in hand with signs of fragmentation; or to rephrase Thorsten Sellin: there is a real risk that criminology's kings ánd queens come to occupy too many different countries and, as a result, tend to lose track of what binds them all together; or, worse, that they start to erect hard borders. Moreover, as Professor Sparks suggests in *Public Criminology?* – one of the key texts in this whole debate, co-authored with his close colleague Professor Ian Loader – criminology has become, paradoxically, a 'successful failure': the flourishing of the field seems to have coincided with 'a waning influence on public debate and social action'. How, then, can criminology contribute to a better politics of crime and its regulation?

Both challenges – fragmentation and criminology being a 'successful failure' – seem to be somehow inter-related, and have come to be addressed in Professor Sparks' work: What roles does criminology play in contemporary democracies? And what is the glue that binds us together *as criminologists* when we fulfil our civic duties? It is not a coincidence that we have chosen 'Criminology and Democratic Politics' as the central theme of the international conference that preceded this ceremony.

The interest of Professor Sparks in renewing criminology is also reflected in various other collaborative projects that testify to his relentless efforts to enrich criminology and to make it, in the words of David Downes, a real *rendez-*

vous subject. This led to various important publications such as *Criminology and Social Theory* (2000, with David Garland), *Criminal Justice and Political Cultures: National and International Dimensions of Crime Control* (2004, with Tim Newburn) and *Travels of the Criminal Question* (2011, with Dario Melossi and Maximo Sozzo).

Next to initiating debate and offering guidance on criminology's role in public life Professor Sparks has published widely in a broad range of criminological areas, in particular on punishment, crime, insecurity and social theory. Professor Sparks has played a key role in the development of international and comparative penology and the empirical and theoretical study of punishment in general, and imprisonment in particular. His empirical work on imprisonment is exemplified in particular in an early study of the Barlinnie Special Unit in Scotland and his research for the 1996 classic *Prisons and the Problem of Order* (co-authored with Anthony Bottoms and William Hay). From the late 1990s onwards Professor Sparks became one of the world's leading advocates for rethinking the agenda of the study of punishment, building a distinctive 'sociology of punishment'. Professor Sparks was editor-in-chief of *Punishment and Society* and co-edited one of the core texts in this field *The SAGE Handbook of Punishment and Society* (2012, with Jonathan Simon) as well as four volumes on *Punishment* (2015, with Richard Jones).

In his earlier research Professor Richard Sparks paved the way for a more comprehensive understanding of experiences of crime, victimisation and fear of crime.

Professor Sparks obtained his PhD at the University of Cambridge in 1990 with a study titled *Crime, television and social anxiety: moral tales and the place of crime in public life*, followed by *Television and the Drama of Crime*, a book published in 1992.

This early work proved to be the starting point for a continuing interest in and critical analysis of questions of risk, insecurity and fear of crime, both in their personal and political dimensions. This has led to, among some other publications, two more books in which our understanding of crime and feelings of insecurity are scrutinised both in the 'private troubles of everyday life' and in our contemporary late modern societies: *Crime and Social Change in Middle England: Questions of Order in an English Town* (with Evi Girling and Ian Loader) in 1999, followed by an edited volume titled *Crime, Risk and Insecurity: Law and Order in Everyday Life and Political Discourse* in 2000 (with Tim Hope).

In his analysis of everyday experiences of fear of crime, Professor Sparks played a prominent role in the classic debate on the rationality of the fear of crime. Indeed, the observation coming from crime and victim surveys that those (groups) with lower chances to become the victim of crime reported higher levels of fear of crime and vice versa, seems intuitively paradoxical. According to Professor Sparks, fear of crime was mistakenly 'treated as a function of risk' leading to the rationalisation of fear: 'fear is fully "rational" only if its existence is accounted for by an antecedent level of objective risk'. He argued that the relation between the 'reality of a risk' and 'fear of crime' is much more complex, and illustrated this point by referring to the 'fear of flying'. Some of us suffer from a 'fear of flying' and although the risks of flying are 'more precisely calculable than the risks of crime', we either fear or do not fear flying irrespective of these risks. Moreover, 'most of us fly without knowing these calculations precisely'. It led to the conclusion that everyday experiences of fear of crime do not correspond to a calculation of the risk of crime, nor are they 'unreal or unreasonable'.

With respect to the political dimensions of risk, insecurity and fear of crime, Professor Sparks points to what others, much later, described as the absorbing qualities of the fear of crime concept, referring to the metaphor of a 'sponge': fear of crime captures more diffuse anxieties that 'result from representations of the social and physical environment, whose sources are broader than the risk of victimisation as such'. This broader contextualisation of the fear of crime touches upon both representations of crime in television, media, public opinion and politics, and the importance of local networks of 'rumour and gossip'.

In the introduction to the aforementioned volume *Crime, Risk and Insecurity*, Richard Sparks and Tim Hope explicitly point to the importance of drawing together the 'concrete, particular and everyday experiences of anxiety about crime' and 'their relations with the emergent forms of criminal justice politics and practice and other contemporary mechanisms of security'. Identifying connections between local and individual experiences of crime in everyday life and broader societal transformations – as documented and analysed by Ulrich Beck, Anthony Giddens, Zygmunt Bauman and other sociologists of our late modern risk society – characterises the work of Professor Sparks; and it is also, and undeniably, an added value for much criminological research. In doing so, Professor Sparks' work revisits and rises to C. Wright Mills' (1959) 'long-standing challenge to the social sciences of understanding the relations between private troubles and public issues', for it is here that the sociological imagination finds it 'most fruitful and demanding applications'.

A final point we would like to mention is Professor Sparks' significant role and contribution to establishing networks and facilitating cooperation within European criminology and beyond. In the light of our celebration of ninety years of criminology in Leuven, we highly value Professor Sparks' active involvement in thinking, discussing and shaping the role and place of a 'public criminology' in contemporary democracies. Professor Sparks is actively involved in LERU, the League of European Research Universities, and the LERU working group on 'Crime and Social Control'. He is co-founder of the Scottish Centre for Crime and Justice Research and was the driving force behind the annual conference of the European Society of Criminology in Edinburgh in 2008. The theme of that European conference was, not coincidentally, 'Criminology in the Public Sphere', referring again to that central question on the role and value of criminology in a democratic society.

Om al deze redenen, Mijnheer de Rector, verzoeken wij u, op voordracht van de Academische Raad, het eredoctoraat van de KU Leuven te verlenen aan Professor Richard Sparks.

Beyond the Rendez-vous

Criminology, Critique, Connection

Richard Sparks

Leuven, 25 April 2019

I could not possibly feel more privileged to be here with you today. To be honoured in this way, in this magnificent place, by this great University, is more to me than I can say. I am acutely conscious that you have chosen to award me this honour as part of the celebrations of ninety years of criminology in Leuven. To be so nominated by colleagues in what is today one of the largest, liveliest, most distinguished and most forward-looking centres of criminology in Europe leaves me astonished. I will say a little today about the history of criminology, though rather more about its possible futures. The time, place and occasion seem apt for this.

We have just had a wonderful conference on the theme of *Criminology and Democratic Politics*. That is also my theme today, and indeed a theme of all my work. Indeed, I have lately become increasingly aware that this was so even before I had articulated it in quite those terms; and I suspect that something similar is true for quite a few people in the field. At that conference were a large proportion of the people with whom I have collaborated throughout my career, and to whom I owe so much, including my co-authors Tony Bottoms, Tim Newburn, Tim Hope, Marion Smith, Máximo Sozzo and of course Ian Loader. I believe deeply in co-operation and co-creation, both as my own preferred way of working and thinking and as principles for building new things; and I will have something further to say about this as well. Indeed, I believe it is not saying too much, nor anticipating my primary point in this paper too far, to say that I see such joint construction and connection-making as central to whatever criminology has to contribute intellectually and practically. Criminology, history, democracy, co-creation, connection – so naturally we begin with fish and chips.

Fish'n'chips is understood (in Britain – I fully understand that this is controversial in Belgium) to be both a deep-rootedly British thing and to be indissolubly linked. Fried battered fish – the kind of fish that really matters when it comes to national identity – was in fact introduced to Britain by Jewish immigrants, probably from Portugal, in the East End of London sometime in the mid-nineteenth century. Frying and battering fish was particularly useful because you could sell it to all-comers on a Friday afternoon and at the same time prepare your own before the start of *Shabbat*. The chip is the more controversial element because it, potentially, has multiple origins – is it Irish or is it indeed Belgian? That the first fish and chip shops in Britain arose on the Lancashire coast in the 1860s does suggest that fried, chipped potatoes entered the UK from Ireland. So, it would appear that fish and chips is the union of a Western Sephardic practice of frying fish in batter or breadcrumbs with an Irish method of cooking potatoes. It is a hybrid of quite recent date. Many, perhaps most, good things are mixtures, to which the idea of purity is alien; but then we commonly forget, or deny, their hybrid character and present them as if they were natural unities.

Now let us think for a moment about the notion of the *rendez-vous* as it appears in the title of my lecture. The use of this metaphor to characterise criminology is widely attributed to David Downes. (I say attributed here advisedly because almost none of the many people who refer to it give a citation; and the most frequently used citation[1] does not in fact contain it. Indeed, having mentioned it ourselves on one or two occasions, I have found that Loader and I are in fact amongst the more frequently nominated sources (I went looking for a reference, and found I was a source)).

More important of course is what we think Downes meant by it, and what we take it to mean. For some this is simply a neat way of saying that criminology is a multi-disciplinary space, informed by a variety of perspectives and answering to a range of different demands. As I understand it, Downes is also more specifically saying that criminology has repeatedly refreshed itself by adopting something from the work of people who do not self-identify as criminologists – they are historians or jurisprudes; sociologists or economists who visit rather

---

1 D. Downes (1988) 'The sociology of crime and social control in Britain, 1960–87', *British Journal of Criminology*, 28/2, *A History of British Criminology*, pp. 45–57.

than inhabit its territory (Durkheim, Foucault, Merton, Goffman, Howard Becker (or Gary Becker), Carol Smart – you name it. Your own preference will shape which of these visitors seem to you most important).[2] Either way, it is a meeting place, a sort of crossroads, a place (to paraphrase Tolkien) of many meetings and many partings. The *rendez-vous* metaphor visualises the never-quite-disciplinary space of criminology as a kind of station concourse. It is a place where people arrange meetings, or simply bump into one another and then go their separate ways, though some of them leave important messages behind.

It is a charming image, of course. In this regard, it well befits the urbanity and deep civility of David Downes himself. It is usually cited in positive terms as expressing something of importance about the plurality of criminology as a field and its receptive, accommodating character. It is also perhaps a way of turning what sometimes feels like a deficit – the chronic absence of the unifying objectives, topics, methods and resources that would serve definitively to constitute criminology as a discipline – to advantage. By extension therefore it is also an argument against what Ian Loader and I have elsewhere called take-over bids – periodic attempts to

[2] On the other hand, it also seems to me that this is not by any means the most interesting thing that Downes himself has to say on the matter. In that same 1988 paper, for example, speaking about the sociology of crime and deviance in UK in the 1970s, Downes remarks: 'It was a dizzying scene, more a paradigmatic kaleidoscope than a clear-cut progression of superior paradigms delivering a knock-out blow to the inferior' (Downes, 1988: 179).

argue that *really* criminology is (or should be henceforth) all about *this*, and hence pursued in *this* way, to *these* ends. We have argued that these attempts to legislate and limit are inherently implausible.[3] In staking a claim to have located the core, they generally do little more than reveal the author's own preferences, usually in manner already glancing backwards by the time it is articulated. They also habitually simplify, reducing the variety of what is *already* there and misrepresenting large chunks of it, whilst foreclosing other new avenues of investigation. Those of us who are attracted by the *rendez-vous* image, by contrast, claim it in aid as an argument for pluralism, and for attentiveness to what is going on in adjacent fields. We prefer to see what we do as part of what the late Richard Ericson called 'a multi-disciplinary, multi-professional, multi-institutional field', not as a discipline *manqué*.[4] In all these ways the *rendez-vous* metaphor has done useful work.

If however we are interested in co-creation and connection, and in the development of these attributes in the interests of stimulating democratic conversation on matters of crime, punishment and regulation then the *rendez-vous* image has its distinct limitations, both intellectually and strategically. It suggests serendipitous

---

[3] I. Loader and R. Sparks (2010) *Public Criminology?*, London: Routledge (chapter 1); I. Loader and R. Sparks (2012) 'Situating criminology' in M. Maguire et al (eds) *The Oxford Handbook of Criminology*, 5th edition, 2012, pp. 3–38.

[4] R. Ericson (2003) 'The Culture and Power of Criminological Research', in L. Zedner and A. Ashworth (eds) *The Criminological Foundations of Penal Policy*, Oxford: Oxford University Press.

meetings, short visits, people bouncing off one another. It does not direct our attention to sustained acts of co-creation or the forging of new connections. Plurality, seen in this way, may be a value, but it is not a purpose. Those who create fruitful new connections – I think here of Pat Carlen[5], for example – do often transgress boundaries insouciantly. They do so in a directed way, however, because they are pursuing a distinct puzzle or project that they cannot adequately develop, as it were, 'inside'.

* * *

Let me now begin to state the argument somewhat more formally. When we consider the history of criminology, we can immediately see the diversity of its origin stories and the differences that exist between its institutional locations and disciplinary connections – coordinates, so to speak, in different national contexts. I will illustrate this briefly in a moment using one example (about Britain) adapted by me from David Garland, and one (about Latin America) borrowed from Máximo Sozzo. This is important because it reminds us of some of the intrinsic reasons for its plural and never-stably-disciplinary character. It is a mixed discourse, at the same time both governmental and critical, always threatening to be pulled back by the gravitational force of state agencies and their practical interests – to collapse into technocracy, so to speak.

---

[5] P. Carlen (2010) *A Criminological Imagination: Essays on Justice, Punishment, Discourse*, London: Routledge.

Yet this very proximity helps explain why criminology has developed an especially vigorous, durable and explicit critical wing, continuously anatomising and exposing the operations of power (their ironies and failures, their perversities and unintended consequences, their rhetorics and alibis) to which it relates.[6]

For these reasons, I think, it remains the case criminology is always threatening to congeal into a discipline with all the associated paraphernalia of rules and benchmarks and well-policed boundaries and a comfortable relation to power. Certainly, it often contains people who are content to inhabit those positions. Yet resistance to this is also permanent, and indeed came into play at an early point in the emergence of the subject. In this sense, criminology's problematic relation to disciplinarity, and its ambivalent orientation towards powerful institutions, are one and the same phenomenon.

Moreover, it is the critiques that draw in the new resources. They raise the normative worries, the historical and comparative reflections, the macro-theories, the reflexive self-interrogation – on which the field depends for growth and contemporary relevance. In this sense critical criminology is not just the 'conscience' of the field – as mainstream criminologists sometimes appear, perhaps rather patronisingly, to grant[7] – it is its

---

[6] D. Garland and R. Sparks (2000) 'Criminology, social theory and the challenge of our times', in D. Garland and R. Sparks (eds) *Criminology and Social Theory*, Oxford: Oxford University Press.

[7] The idea of the critical as the 'conscience' of the 'professional' also appears in Michael Burawoy's famous article 'For Public Sociology'

intellectual crucible, and the source of much of its energy and capacity for change (a point emphasised repeatedly, and I think convincingly, by the late Jock Young).[8] Perhaps then the *rendez-vous*, in addition to its other difficulties, is too anodyne an image, in that it understates *not just* the ferocity of the debates and the gravity of what is at stake in them (and hence their permanent character) but also their capacity for fusion and creativity.

For these reasons, to reach *beyond* the *rendez-vous* idea is to remind ourselves that criminology tends to be at its most creative when its defences are down, and when it reaches outside for refreshment and orientation. At such moments its governmental and critical imperatives can on occasion travel some distance together because they seek to respond to the grand challenges presented to them by the changing predicaments of the exterior world rather than focusing on their membership of different factions. It ceases to be a passive receiver. It is not just a site for the meeting of other influences, a place marked by the passage of various distinguished visitors. Neither is it something entire and self-contained. We can begin to think less about 'criminological theories' (a fairly limited and banal set, when all's said and done) and more about theorising as an activity. We can think much less about criminology's internal squabbles and more about its

---

(*American Sociological Review*, 70: 1, pp. 4–28, 2005), misleadingly according to Loader and myself, amongst others.

[8] For example J. Young (2002) 'Critical criminology in the twenty-first century: critique, irony and the always unfinished', in K. Carrington and R. Hogg (eds) *Critical Criminology: Issues, Debates, Challenges*, Cullompton: Willan Publishing.

capacity to engage with and participate in other conversations. In so doing we can resist becoming insulated from the wider currents of sociological, legal, psychological and other traditions of thought that originally animated criminology and constituted it as a point of intersection and creativity.[9] If we want to *create* new hybrids that have lasting effects – our own fish and chips perhaps – then what matters is not the encounter but the *liaison* that follows it.

* * *

Why does this matter, particularly now? One reason is that criminology is probably better equipped to make a bid for disciplinary glory now than at any time in the past, for reasons that Loader and I have discussed elsewhere at some length.[10] Yet this would occur precisely at a moment when the scope and diversity of the problems of crime, regulation and control in the world, their protean capacity to shift and mutate, their complete involvement with technological change and new cultural forms and conflicts, environmental threats, questions of war and peace, make any such move disastrously irrelevant. Moreover, disciplinary settlements tend to exclude certain kinds of questions, especially normative and evaluative ones. The English social theorist Andrew Sayer argues that since both social scientists and those

---

[9] D. Garland (2011) 'Criminology's Place in the Academic Field', in M. Bosworth and C. Hoyle (eds) *What is Criminology?*, Oxford: Oxford University Press.

[10] I. Loader and R. Sparks (2010) *Public Criminology?*, London: Routledge.

whom they study are 'evaluative beings' we cannot drive considerations of normative value out of our work without mis-recognising what is at stake.[11] Our relation to the world, he says, is 'one of concern'. We are sentient creatures who can flourish or suffer, and we need a social science that does justice to this aspect of social being. Sayer argues that social science perspectives that strive to be adequate to the study of evaluative being tend to be post-disciplinary, and in this respect to resemble and recall the *pre*-disciplinary conversations of their eighteenth and nineteenth century antecedents.

In this sense my primary point, like Sayer's, is not one about inter-, or pre- or post- disciplinarity. Criminology *is* irremediably interdisciplinary, thank goodness – but it is hardly alone in that. Most interesting and relevant knowledge-formations are. Nor is it mainly to assert that it needs to be so in order to either explain or interpret the world, though it clearly does. All criminology's objects are overdetermined. It is a hybrid discourse, addressed to hybrid things. The point is rather what uses we wish to make of these properties and how they benefit the development of what Loader and I elsewhere call 'a better politics of crime'.

One particular mission I want to claim for criminology beyond the *rendez-vous* is as a connector, a linker-upper, a maker and facilitator of *liaisons*. In order to develop this point I am going to refer to two definitions of the

---

[11] A. Sayer (2011) *Why Things Matter to People*, Cambridge: Cambridge University Press (chapter 1).

idea of pragmatism. One of these is somewhat limiting and incurious. This is what Stanley Cohen had in mind when he alluded to 'pragmatic frame of reference' that he attributed to British criminology before the explosion of critical discourse in the 1970s – what he saw as a piecemeal, restrictive, problem-solving, eclectic and largely atheoretical orientation, absolutely ripe for the disruption that the radicals brought to it.[12] This is also very much what Tim Hope and I meant in alluding to the notion of a 'pragmatic criminology' in a paper that we wrote some twenty years ago on the claims and limits of situational crime prevention.[13] I want to contrast with this the value as I see it – and which is the key theme of recent work by Ian Loader and myself – of the pragmatist tradition in political philosophy, and especially its encouragement of *inquiry* as a participatory and inclusive activity.

I think there is good reason to argue that pragmatism in the latter sense is a philosophical tradition that has a particular affinity with criminology as a field, and especially with a criminology that is understood – in the way that I would urge that we understand it – as a post-disciplinary, critical, egalitarian, connective and fully contemporary thematic space. In other words, the value of criminology's hybridity is to enable and stimulate

---

[12] S. Cohen (1988) *Against Criminology*, London: Transaction Publishers.

[13] T. Hope and R. Sparks (2000) 'For a social theory of situations: or how useful is pragmatic criminology?' in A. von Hirsch et al (eds) *Ethical and Social Perspectives on Situational Crime Prevention*, Oxford: Hart Publishing.

discourse, to promote conversation, and to connect distant and mutually separated settings and lives, and thereby to promote unanticipated solutions, to mediate conflict and misunderstanding and to serve the extension of democratic imagination and empathy.

These two senses of pragmatism, therefore, capture something of importance about the duality of criminology – its applications and its aspirations, its realism (another contested term) and its utopian moments, the ever-present tug of instrumentalism and the prospect of richer and fuller democratic deliberation.

Quite often in recent times criminology has seemed not just pragmatic in the former, limiting sense but downright disappointed, preoccupied with its own failures, its most notable practitioners frequently convinced of its impossibility, divided between bombastic technocrats and dejected critics.[14] For many of the latter the sheer scale and obduracy of the phenomenon of mass incarceration in the United States and its echoes and sequels elsewhere induced despair, so that critical discourse became increasingly focused on the diagnosis of everything that had gone terribly wrong and the enumeration of obstacles to change. Inequality and

---

[14] See further I. Loader and R. Sparks (2012) 'Beyond Lamentation: towards a democratic egalitarian politics of crime and justice', in T. Newburn and J. Peay (eds) *Policing: Politics, Culture and Control. Essays in Honour of Robert Reiner*, Oxford: Hart Publishing, pp. 11–41; and I. Loader and R. Sparks (2019) 'Democratic experimentalism and the futures of crime control: resources of hope for demotic times', in P. Carlen and L. Ayres França (eds) *Justice Alternatives*, London: Routledge.

insecurity stoked incarceration. State incapacity generated the insincerity of hype, masking the reality of persistent ineffectiveness. I want to suggest that a refocusing on the possibilities of pragmatism in the second sense might lead us in the direction of a different and more hopeful vocabulary, one organised around the principle of connection – intersection, interstices, interaction, intervention.

* * *

Curiously, how we think about the history of criminology, especially the history of theory, has an important part to play in reorienting its future.

As Garland has emphasised criminology as a field of empirical inquiry characteristically begins with concerns arising from practice. It is for this reason that Garland long ago argued that penology precedes, and provides the generative context for, the development of criminology as a wider field of inquiry.[15] Thus, for example in the United Kingdom the scientific, clinical and reformist interests of a wide range of practitioners, but initially perhaps especially psychiatrists and social workers, long pre-dated the development of research institutes, or university degree programmes, or conferences devoted to the promotion of criminology as a 'subject'.

---

[15] D. Garland (1985) 'The criminal and his science: A Critical Account of the Formation of Criminology at the End of the Nineteenth Century', *British Journal of Criminology*, 25/2: 109-137.

The formation of criminological discourse in Britain thus includes a wide range of disparate influences. It involves the activities of a range of movements for social reform and 'improvement' alongside the widespread and intensifying attachment of respectable opinion throughout the later 19th and early 20th centuries to science. It also arises out of the specific development of a range of institutions and practices aimed at correcting the habits, morals and lifestyles of the disreputable poor. Emblematic here are such innovations as the Probation of Offenders Act (1907) with its resonant injunction to 'advise, assist and befriend' the wayward, the 'delinquent', the inebriated.[16]

In its articulations with the emergent 'penal-welfare complex' criminology in Britain thus begins both within and outside 'the state'. These pluralist and interventionist characteristics help to explain why there has never been a predominance either of Beccarian 'Classicism' nor of programmatic Positivism in British criminology despite its attachments to science and its proximity to clinical practices. Neither do the textbook oppositions between such 'paradigms' very well describe its eclectic, pragmatic, empiricist and reformist preferences.

At least one mid-20th century European émigré liked what he saw. Leon Radzinowicz, in an autobiography published as late as 1999, recalls his attraction to English political culture as he encountered it in and after the

[16] D. Garland (1985) *Punishment and Welfare: A History of Penal Strategies*, Aldershot: Gower; D. Garland (1988) 'British Criminology before 1935', *British Journal of Criminology*, 28/2: 1–17.

1930s. It was, in his eyes, 'down to earth, practical, observant, critical'.[17] 'England', he asserts, 'made me a realist and a pragmatist'.

The influence of Radzinowicz on the subsequent development of the subject was distinctive and substantial but nowadays culturally remote. Radzinowicz set out to create an academic field in the image of the virtues that he attributed to British institutions – thoroughness, decency, probity and a lack of ideological enthusiasm.[18]

Yet even if Cohen's 'pragmatic frame of reference' seen as characterising these institutions was initially dominant, it did not take long for it to receive certain significant shocks and challenges. Indeed, criminology rapidly became a focal site for the political and intellectual debates and conflicts that gripped British society in the 1960s. A new generation of social scientists, embarking on academic careers in newly founded universities brought new objects of enquiry to the fore: deviance, social control, political conflict and state violence, police power, ideology and the manufacture of news, not to mention the reflexive and intentionally subversive re-examination of the claims and effects of criminology itself.[19]

---

[17] L. Radzinowicz (1999) *Adventures in Criminology*, London: Routledge.

[18] T. Newburn (2011) 'Criminology and Government: Some reflections on recent developments in England', in M. Bosworth and C. Hoyle (eds.) *What is Criminology?*, Oxford: Oxford University Press.

[19] For a slightly more extended rendition of this argument see J. Savelsberg, L.A. Hughes, J. Kivivuori, J.F. Short Jr., M. Sozzo and R. Sparks 'Criminology, History of', in *International Encyclopedia of Social and Behavioral Sciences*, 2nd edition, Amsterdam: Elsevier, 2015.

New theoretical perspectives and concepts took centre stage: appreciation, labeling, moral panics, symbolic interactionism, anti-psychiatry, Marxism and feminism. New institutions were assembled to provide a platform for these perspectives and to build alliances with radical social workers and lawyers, students, prisoners' organisations and campaigns against state violence. Foremost among these were the National Deviancy Conference (1968–1979) and the European Group for the Study of Deviance and Social Control (founded in 1973 and still in existence). The small, somewhat insular, rather a-theoretical world of 'mainstream' British criminology had been subverted almost as soon as it had been established.

The resulting ironies and fissures are never far to seek in the subsequent development of criminology as a 'discipline'. As Cohen further observes: 'The more successful our attacks on the old regime, the more we received PhDs, tenure, publishers' contracts and research funds, appeared on booklists and examination questions, and even became directors of institutes of criminology'. Criminology in Britain as elsewhere exhibits a permanent duality, as both a critical and a governmental discourse[20], and continues to invite takeover bids and denunciations from partisans on either side. Its relationship to government and public policy remains integral, yet unlikely ever to recapture the intimacy, or easy alignment of world-views, that characterised its birth.

[20] D. Garland and R. Sparks (2000) 'Criminology, social theory and the challenge of our times', in D. Garland and R. Sparks (eds) *Criminology and Social Theory*, Oxford: Oxford University Press.

At around the same time, as Sozzo shows,[21] criminology in Latin America was born when ideas of the Italian "Positivist School" were imported in the 1880s. The biological emphasis of Italian positivism rapidly came under challenge from scholars who began to stress the psychological and sociological dimensions of crime causation. Most prominent among these scholars was Jose Ingenieros. Sozzo reports that from the turn of the twentieth century onwards schools of criminology sometimes came into being, as in Argentina, in direct affiliation with police and prison institutions. For example, in 1907 the Institute of Criminology was created within the National Penitentiary of Buenos Aires, and Ingenieros was appointed its first director. Ingenieros thus looks like a rather emblematic figure, not least in the contradictions that he embodies – a communist and a civil servant; a social reformer working within the context of a penal institution.[22]

If we jump forward several decades we can similarly see that subsequent 'waves' of criminology in Latin America also emerge both through absorption of ideas from other places – the United States, Italy, for example – and in response to social and political changes, upheavals and conflicts 'at home'. *Translation*, in all of its plural senses is thus of critical importance, not merely in the obvious

---

21 In Savelsberg et al, *op. cit.*

22 See also M.B. Plotkin (2016) 'José Ingenieros, *El Hombre Mediocre*, and Social Integration in Turn-of-the-20th-Century Argentina', *Oxford Research Encyclopaedias Online, Latin American History*: http://oxfordre.com/latinamericanhistory/view/10.1093/acrefore/9780199366439.001.0001/acrefore-9780199366439-e-346.

guise of the translation of texts from English or Italian into Spanish or Portuguese, but also in the work of movement – the literal *carrying across* of ideas between contexts and circumstances.[23]

Sozzo reports that since the 1980s in response to processes of democratisation throughout most of Latin America criminology has undergone an opening towards social science and critical theory. It has also undertaken a profound questioning both of its relation to state institutions and to the dominance of English-language criminology, preoccupied with problems and perspectives defined on the projection of the Global North. In that process – paradoxically yet characteristically – as criminological research has flourished and diversified, so the label "criminology" (designating a distinct, institutionalised academic field) has ceased to exercise exclusive jurisdiction over problems of crime, justice and social control. Thus, Sozzo argues, "the field of studies assumed, during these last twenty years, a polyvalent and complex structure", involving "strong contradictions and debates" and "substantial challenges regarding both knowledge production and policy relevance". It has also become a major driver in what may turn out to be the most significant reorientation of the field thus far in the twenty-first century, namely the emergence of an inclusive and consciously counter-colonial *Southern* Criminology.[24]

---

[23] See further D. Melossi, M. Sozzo and R. Sparks (2011) 'Criminal questions: cultural embeddedness and global mobilities' in D. Melossi et al (eds) *Travels of the Criminal Question*, Oxford: Hart Publishing.

[24] K. Carrington, R. Hogg, J. Scott, M. Sozzo and R. Walters (2018) *Southern Criminology*, London: Routledge.

This brief excursus into the historical development of criminology in two very divergent (but never entirely disconnected) contexts has, I think, established several points of importance to the argument I wish to develop here. It tells us something, I think, about the complex responsiveness between the development of criminological discourse and the intellectual and political settings of its emergence. It reminds us that the spaces that criminology occupies are inherently incapable of being insulated from 'external' influences and hence that aspirations towards paradigmatic unity and legislative stipulations of what criminology comprises are entirely unfeasible, indeed alien to its very history. Thirdly, it suggests that criminology tends to combine – uneasily but persistently – both governmental and critical dimensions. The governmental dimension – so often, and frequently with justification, castigated by critics as limiting criminology's horizons, compromising its autonomy, drawing it into complicity with power – is itself ambiguous, being carried forward by actors who self-identify (no doubt with varying degrees of justification) as standing at the leading edge of social change.

There are however powerful influences that tend to want to restrict criminology's scope and ambition and to sever its connection with critique. Their predominant mode – certainly in the British case and I suspect elsewhere too – is to emphasise its pragmatic aspect, in the first (restrictive) sense. The seduction and reduction here is the one that Tim Hope and I had in mind in our little paper, now so long ago. It says that criminology is most useful when it settles for just-good-enough theory in order to guide immediate practical applications. It encourages the approach that Ian Loader once aptly termed 'jobbing' criminology.[25] It depicts criminology as a fixer-upper discourse – handy, biddable and ideologically non-committal. Yet this is not all that pragmatism is, not by a very long way indeed.

* * *

So far I have argued that criminology is irredeemably plural in its sources and that this should encourage an active, outward-looking, responsive and worldly sensibility. Its hybridity is original to it and attempts to police its borders or to stipulate its content limit and constrain the contributions it may yet make to responding to the world and its troubles. A proper reading of criminology's history – its very different national and regional histories – suggests that the governmental and critical impulses within it have both been present all along. The tension between these is very real and centrally important. That tension will never be permanently resolved in one direction or the other, or so we must hope.

Re-describing criminology as a discipline – however tempting this may be given that it increasingly acquires all the accoutrements of one – does not help. Sayer's observation that contemporary post-disciplinarity in

[25] I. Loader (1998) 'Criminology and the public sphere: arguments for a utopian realism', in P. Walton and J. Young *The New Criminology Revisited*, London: Palgrave Macmillan.

some ways looks a lot like the pre-disciplinary questing curiosity of the early social sciences is more useful. In this light, Downes's widely cited idea that criminology is a *rendez-vous* subject takes us so far, but not far enough. Ironically, the most interesting way I can see of resisting the pull of those forces that would reduce criminology to its governmental, technocratic side alone – and hence accomplish the dominance of pragmatic criminology – is by exploring the meanings of pragmatism.

In the remainder of this paper I will develop the argument that the post-disciplinary future of criminology lies in actively seeking to convene and facilitate new kinds of connections and conversations. These include conversations between exponents of different disciplines, of course. However, they include many other actors as well. Some of these are quite familiar. They are the tricky but well-known transactions between scholars, criminal justice practitioners, policy-makers, activists, journalists, social media opinion-formers and others that compose the public culture of societies of the Global North today. Those have been described many times, and were in some part the back-drop to the work that Loader and I undertook in *Public Criminology?*.[26] Some such conversations require extending the circles of participation to encompass others

[26] I. Loader and R. Sparks (2010) *Public Criminology?*, London: Routledge. From this point on the argument of the paper draws extensively on work jointly conducted with Ian Loader, and my collaboration with him has been a central part of my working life for about the last twenty-five years – something for which I feel immensely lucky and grateful. For this reason, and because so many of the views

who have not generally been party to such debates – and I will return to the implications of this for questions of the scope and ambition of these ideas in conclusion.

Pragmatism in this context refers to a tradition of political thought that places the model of a conversation at the centre of its understanding of *inquiry*, and inquiry at the centre of its hopes for the development of democracy. If we want criminology to be more than a technocratic discourse, but also more than a site of rendez-vous, then one of the things it needs to be is an instigator of those kinds of conversations.

* * *

At the end of our book *Public Criminology?* Loader and I suggested that one of the aspirations of students of crime and punishment (criminologists for want of a better term) should be to help create the conditions for a better politics of crime. Criminologists' special contribution to that objective, we suggested, took the form of trying to raise the prevailing quality of political argument about crime and social ordering. The ways in which they do this, we suggested, include but are certainly not limited to those of correcting misinformation, weighing evidence about existing policies and practices, and designing alternative interventions. Those certainly do seem to us to be basic, indeed central, obligations for social scientists; and the rigour, persistence and respect for evidence with

---

expressed here were arrived at jointly, I will wherever relevant use the first-person plural. This really is about what we think, not just me.

which they are pursued are central to what distinguishes their investigation as topics for social science, in quality if not in kind, from other kinds of opinion.

However, these objectives, extremely demanding though they clearly are, do not seem to us to be quite enough to capture either all the specific responsibilities upon or the opportunities open to people working on problems of crime and punishment. The alternative conception that we presented there involved cultivating a set of practices and dispositions that we called 'democratic under-labouring'.

Although we were quite roundly criticised by some reviewers for not saying enough about what we thought the better politics of crime might look like, we did have a few things to say by way of orientation. And we went on in subsequent work to express the view that:

> 'Any discussion of the criminal question encodes in miniature a set of claims about the nature of the good society, and any attempt to answer it – however apparently 'dry', technical, or limited in scope – carries and projects a possible world, a desirable state of affairs that a political or criminological author wishes to recover, preserve, or usher into existence.'[27]

One aspect of the democratic under-labourer's work, we thought, was to assist in developing 'a more hopeful and

---

[27] See further I. Loader and R. Sparks (2012) 'Beyond Lamentation', in T. Newburn and J. Peay (eds) *Policing: Politics, Culture and Control (Essays in Honour of Robert Reiner)*, Oxford: Hart Publishing.

more richly democratic way of approaching questions of crime and justice'.[28] We have gone on to argue that by contrast with its facility in empirical methods and policy analysis, criminology's understanding of surrounding political contexts, and in particular its sensitivity to normative conceptual discussion – what we came to term its *political frame of evaluation* – are less developed.[29] We should no longer accept this limitation, we argued. To do so often seems like an undefended desire to somehow *replace* politics with what Bruno Latour calls "calculative devices".[30] We can no longer consider expertise as in some way an antidote to democratic politics. Instead, we need to think afresh about criminology's relation to problems, and promises, of democracy. It is simply part of our job to reflect upon the bearing that institutions and political structures have on criminal justice, and on how these might change.

Amongst the consequences of thinking along these lines, we argued, would be a clearer sense of the need for "argumentative"[31] or "intelligent"[32] rather than simply "evidence-based" public policy-making. Crime and

---

[28] *Op. cit.*

[29] I. Loader and R. Sparks (2016) 'Ideologies and crime: political ideas and the dynamics of crime control', *Global Crime*, DOI: 10.1080/17440572.2016.1169926.

[30] B. Latour (2004) *Politics of Nature: How to bring the sciences into democracy*, Cambridge: Cambridge University Press.

[31] R. Hoppe (1999) 'Policy analysis, science and politics: From "speaking truth to power" to "making sense together"', *Science and Public Policy*, 26/3: 201–10.

[32] I. Sanderson (2009) 'Intelligent policy making for a complex world: pragmatism, evidence and learning', *Political Studies*, 57: 699–719.

punishment are special topics in many ways, including the intensity of the passions that they often arouse, and the special considerations of criminal law that constitute them. Nonetheless, criminology is in no sense alone in these respects, all of which partake of widespread features of the relationships between scientific discourses, policy and public participation in the world we now inhabit.

On this view criminology is committed both to participating within, and to facilitating and extending, institutional spaces that supplement representative politics with inclusive public deliberation about crime and justice matters, whether in local, state, or national arenas – or across emergent transnational spaces. In giving this disposition a name – that of democratic under-labouring (we quite accept could have been catchier) we certainly did not imagine that we were inventing anything, let alone stipulating how everyone ought to behave. We did and do believe, however, that it was a fairly apt way of trying to draw out some key features of the practices of many thoughtful and engaged people for whom it is an important challenge to try to reconcile an earnest commitment to scholarship and knowledge-generation with an equally sincere and sustained desire to change the world.

So, what kind of democrat is the democratic under-labourer? What is their contribution to intelligent, argumentative public deliberation? Which kinds of political thinking best support and develop our understanding of the relations between expert knowledge and democratic participation?

In their recent extension of accounts of legitimacy in criminal justice, Tony Bottoms and Justice Tankebe argue that legitimacy is best thought of as a matter of ongoing dialogue. It involves, they suggest, a continual dynamic of claim and response, and is thus 'more like a perpetual discussion' than a single assertion of power or command.[33]

We think this is an important insight, but one whose implications we need to press further if we are to fully gather its implications for the development of a better politics of crime. We would argue that, more especially, it also has to do with contemporary people's expectations of voice or participation in important public questions that affect their lives.

It is this view that I intend to develop here and in future work with regard to the insights of the pragmatist tradition in political theory.

* * *

Pragmatism as a living tradition is of course many things, but in the sense intended here it is a body of political thought committed to discovery and experimentation as collective, participatory activities. The central contributor to whom I will refer here is John Dewey, though other important democratic thinkers past and present

[33] A. Bottoms and J. Tankebe (2012) 'Beyond Procedural Justice: A Dialogic Approach to Legitimacy in Criminal Justice', *The Journal of Criminal Law and Criminology*, 102/1: 101–150.

(including Albert Hirschman, Roberto Unger, Amy Gutman, Cheryl Misak, Hilary Putnam and Richard Rorty) are also key voices within it. Pragmatism is *par excellence* the body of work whose central concerns include reconciling the place of specialist, expert knowledge with an ambitious, participatory and egalitarian conception of democratic citizenship. It thus seems odd that it has played so little explicit role in the development of criminology, especially by contrast with its influence elsewhere in the social sciences. (One thinks most obviously Dewey's influence in education and Hirschman's in political science). Criminology, as a hybrid, governmental-critical, connective set of discourses ought to be fertile ground for this perspective, one might think. That it should become so now, is the central argument here.

Dewey understands 'inquiry' as 'the transformation of an indeterminate situation' into one that we are able to comprehend more fully and confidently.[34] Dewey expressly rejects the supposed superiority of what he terms the 'spectator theory of knowledge' but not, crucially, the growth of knowledge as such. On the contrary he affirms that democratic dialogue is the 'precondition for the full application of intelligence to the solution of social problems'.[35] Inquiry in this sense is reflexive, continuous and collective. The object of inquiry

---

[34] J. Dewey (1938). *Logic: The theory of inquiry*, in J.A. Boydston (ed) (2008) *John Dewey: The later works, 1925 – 1953*, Carbondale: Southern Illinois University Press, 2nd edition.

[35] H. Putnam (1990) 'A Reconsideration of Deweyian Democracy', *Southern California Law Review*, 63: 1671–1697.

is an 'inevitably provisional solution to the practical and intellectual problem that sparked inquiry'.[36] 'Inquiry' in this sense is something undertaken collectively by actors seeking solutions to problems: 'part of an existential struggle to cope with an objectively precarious but improvable environment.'

A particular kind of aspiration thus underpins this conception. This is that a process of inquiry, inviting participation by all who are affected by a problem or decision, sets in train a momentum towards democratic development. Democracy, says Dewey, is 'a way of personal life controlled not merely by faith in human nature in general but by faith in the capacity of human beings for intelligent judgement and action if proper conditions are furnished'.[37]

Dewey wrote these words late in his long life, on the threshold of a political upheaval far greater even than those we confront today. He cleaved to the view that only the renewal and deepening of democracy could begin to confront the challenges of the time:

> 'The depth of the present crisis is due in considerable part to the fact that for a long period we acted as if our democracy were something that perpetuated itself automatically; as if

[36] 'Dewey's political philosophy' in Stanford Encyclopedia of Philosophy (2005): https://plato.stanford.edu/entries/dewey-political/.

[37] J. Dewey (1939) 'Creative Democracy: The Task Before Us', available at: https://www.philosophie.uni-muenchen.de/studium/das_fach/warum_phil_ueberhaupt/dewey_creative_democracy.pdf.

> our ancestors had succeeded in setting up a machine that solved the problem of perpetual motion in politics.'[38]

In Dewey's view of the world, robust experimental inquiry and open democratic conversation are inseparable – neither can thrive without the other. It is a conception that speaks to the texture of everyday life, and to every level of institutions. It is a conception that is oriented to experimentation, discovery, refinement and self-correction, certainly (and in these senses, centrally to 'fallibilism'). It is, equally importantly, organised around principles of participation, mutual recognition and unconstrained discussion. At its heart is not 'the political machine' but the conversation itself: 'the strongest point to be made in behalf of even such rudimentary political forms as democracy has attained, popular voting, majority rule and so on, is that to some extent they involve a consultation and discussion which concerns social needs and troubles'.[39]

Here and now, in a moment of well-founded fear, we need to hear this. We are surrounded by reasons to be dubious about democracy – to fear for it, certainly, but also sometimes to want to tame it. We have special reason to worry about these things in respect of crime and punishment, when the powers and passions at stake are so utterly fateful. We rightly often want to defend the

[38] *Idem.*

[39] J. Dewey (1929) *The Public and its Problems,* in J.A. Boydston (ed) (2008) *John Dewey: The later works, 1925 – 1953,* Carbondale: Southern Illinois University Press, 2nd edition.

claims of expertise and rationality against the rantings of the populists and the manipulations of propagandists.[40] It is tempting to resort to a more defensive posture – to try to insulate the things we value from the surrounding noise. Dewey urges us to turn towards democratisation, not to withdraw from it. As one of his inheritors Richard Bernstein argues, Dewey's creative democracy is 'the task still before us'.[41]

* * *

There seems a great deal more to say. Yet is it is time to conclude, at least for today.

I began by arguing that criminology is not just a meeting place (though it is that). It is not just a point of intersections between disciplines, theories or methods (though it is all of these). It is something that lives in a tense, ambiguous space – simultaneously governmental and critical, pragmatic and utopian. No wonder it can be a bit fractious at times.

I think that since these conundrums can't be solved, they should be put to use.

I went on to argue that criminology should resist the recurrent pull to resolve its inner tension in favour of the governmental pole, and to become in the negative sense

---

[40] I. Loader and R. Sparks (2017) 'Penal populism and epistemic crime control' in A. Liebling et al (eds) *The Oxford handbook of Criminology*, 6th edition, Oxford: Oxford University Press.

[41] R.J. Bernstein (2000) 'Creative Democracy – The Task Still Before Us', *American Journal of Theology & Philosophy* 21/3: 215–228.

of the term more pragmatic. One way of doing this is to explore its relations with pragmatism as a tradition of democratic political theory. That turns out to offer a completely different kind of invitation – namely to think afresh about inquiry and problem-solving as opportunities for radical, inclusive democratic experimentation. Rejecting pragmatic criminology in favour of pragmatism only sounds paradoxical at first.

The idea of the *rendez-vous* (as useful as it has been) doesn't take us far enough in this direction. It does not capture the active, conscious, effortful work of connection that seems important now.[42] At the heart of this idea is an image of conversation – of many kinds of conversations, in many venues – because that is central to the work of inquiry in the Deweyan sense.

Standing here in Leuven, in the heartland of European restorative justice theory and research, it may be that none of this sounds particularly surprising. Restorative justice at its heart similarly concerns the work of particular forms of conversation, and the opportunities they present to resolve problematic situations and allow people to move forward. Some of this work speaks to the immediate situational elements of encounters – their ritual aspects and conversational dynamics.[43] I think this is crucially important for a number of practical,

---

[42] D. Allen (2004) *Talking to Strangers*, Chicago: University of Chicago Press.

[43] For example N. Harris, L. Walgrave and J. Braithwaite (2004) 'Emotional Dynamics in Restorative Conferences', *Theoretical Criminology*, 8(2), 191–210.

theoretical and ethical reasons, and some work that I have undertaken jointly with Evi Girling and Marion Smith also speaks to these concerns.[44]

Of course, this tradition has also evolved far beyond these starting points to include urgent, collective problems – peace agreements, truth commissions, transitional justice arrangements. John Braithwaite's work is central here; and as he has recently indicated there are major conceptual and practical challenges involved in the task of 'scaling up' restorative justice.[45] No doubt all efforts to extend deliberation confront similar challenges when they move beyond the level of the immediate scene of face-to-face discussion. Yet we also know that there are ways, some in-person, some (increasingly) online, of extending those opportunities: crowdsourcing, 'preferenda', citizens' juries, consensus conferences, citizens' assemblies, to name a few.

I suspect therefore that pragmatist-inspired democratic theory and restorative justice have important things to learn from one another. As a number of scholars including Braithwaite[46] and Albert Dzur[47] have made

---

[44] M. Smith, E. Girling and R. Sparks (2000) 'Educating Sensibilities: The Image of "The Lesson" in Children's Talk about Punishment', *Punishment & Society*, 2(4), 395–415.

[45] J. Braithwaite (2016) 'Learning to Scale up Restorative Justice' in K. Clamp (ed) *Restorative Justice in Transitional Settings,* 173–189, Abingdon: Routledge.

[46] J. Braithwaite (2015) 'Deliberative Republican Hybridity through Restorative Justice', *Raisons Politiques* 59(3), 33–49.

[47] A. Dzur (2015) 'Public Restorative Justice: The Participatory Democratic Dimensions of Institutional Reform', *Raisons Politiques* 59(3), 51–71.

clear, restorative justice is one among several portals, so to speak, between the worlds of criminology and democratisation. Indeed, Braithwaite's later work makes clear that the primary relevance of deliberative work does not lie in process of adjudication within criminal justice at all, as important as these are, but in building spaces for problem-solving and peace-building under stressed and conflictual circumstances.

As Bottoms and Tankebe's views on the dialogic character of legitimacy in contemporary societies clearly imply, procedures alone probably hold no solution to the current legitimation problems of criminal justice institutions.[48] Loader and I suggest elsewhere[49], following Pierre Rosanvallon[50], that contemporary requirements for public legitimacy almost inevitably include forms of 'proximity', recognition and emotional intelligence. In this sense, the paradox of an allegedly anti-political age is that it continually generates demands for rights of participation, even if actually securing people's

---

[48] The converse is also clearly untrue, however – sacrificing the protections of due process in the interests of satisfying some inchoate public 'demand' is highly unlikely to achieve any desirable effect, let alone restore lost public confidence.

[49] Loader and Sparks (2019) 'Democratic experimentalism and the futures of crime control: resources of hope for demotic times', in P. Carlen and L. Ayres França (eds) *Justice Alternatives*, London: Routledge. See also I. Loader and R. Sparks (2013) 'Unfinished business: legitimacy, crime control and democratic politics', in J. Tankebe and A. Liebling (eds) *Legitimacy and Criminal Justice*, Oxford: Oxford University Press.

[50] P. Rosanvallon (2011) *Democratic Legitimacy: Impartiality, Reflexivity, Proximity*, Princeton: Princeton University Press.

engagement in democratic processes is another, altogether patchier and more problematic matter. Pragmatist democratic theory since Dewey has placed participation, and access to deliberative opportunities over matters that concern people centre-stage, something that the more statist and otherwise 'pragmatic' forms of criminological theory and research have often been too ready to sacrifice or ignore. It insists, moreover, that such commitments are preferable *epistemically*, and not only as matters of taste. We cannot be serious about our own beliefs, Cheryl Misak argues, unless we are prepared to test them in dialogue with the beliefs and experiences of others.[51] We are compelled, she says, to attend to others and to do our best to render decision-making mechanisms as inclusive as possible.[52]

None of this is to deny that specialist knowledge is a vital constituent in democratic decision-making. Yet the idea of expert knowledge alone as decisive is inherently dubious. Dewey famously asserted that: 'A class of experts is inevitably so removed from common interests as to become a class with private interests and private knowledge, which in social matters is not knowledge at all.'[53] Listening is a central democratic virtue, and a quality that scholars and experts (the very people whose

---

[51] C. Misak (2000) *Truth, Politics, Morality: Pragmatism and Deliberation*, London: Routledge, p. 94.

[52] C. Misak, *op. cit.*, p. 127. See also R. Westbrook (2005) *Democratic Hope: Pragmatism and the Politics of Truth*, Cornell University Press.

[53] J. Dewey (1927) 'The Public and its Problems', in J.A. Boydston (ed) (2008) *John Dewey: The later works, 1925 – 1953*, Carbondale: Southern Illinois University Press, 2nd edition.

social position Dewey feared made them least inclined to attend to others) particularly need to cultivate.[54]

These are among the concerns that I had in mind at the outset in arguing that criminology can actively seek more diverse and creative connections. They are connections across disciplines, contexts and other boundaries. Clifford Shearing and Cameron Holley, setting out the scale of the intellectual and political challenges confronting scholarship in the face of climate change, habitat destruction and ecocide, make a similar point. To rise to those challenges is certainly to seek new connections and to acknowledge our obligations to those living far away or yet unborn. It is also to set aside restrictions imposed by any sense of disciplinary boundedness. The tasks before us are too great for such trivia.[55]

Having few if any defensible boundaries itself, criminology can make a virtue of its porosity and its hybridity, as at its best it has often done. It need not wait for visitors to pass through. It can start more conversations, listen more attentively, experiment more adventurously; and in so doing it can realise more of its promise as a critical as well as a governmental discourse, a modest but resolute labourer for democracy after all.

---

[54] L. Bassell (2017) *The Politics of Listening: Possibilities and Challenges for Democratic Life*, London: Palgrave.

[55] C. Shearing and C. Holley (2018) 'Thriving on a pale blue dot: criminology and the Anthropocene', in C. Shearing and C. Holley (eds) *Criminology and the Anthropocene*, London: Routledge.